Popular Performer

Arranged by CAROL TORNQUIST

The Best Songs of Christmas

While carols are ever present during the Christmas season, popular music has also become an important part of holiday celebrations. This collection revisits classic as well as contemporary favorites, casting them in the rich voice of the piano. Cheerful selections are included, such as "Frosty the Snowman" and "It's the Most Wonderful Time of the Year." There are also heartwarming ballads, including "Grown-Up Christmas List," which was made famous by Amy Grant, and Jim Brickman's "The Gift." The playful swing of "Santa Claus Is Comin' to Town," the sassy stride of "Santa Baby," and all of the other wonderful musical moments are certain to provide hours of enjoyment for the pianist who wishes to be a *Popular Performer*.

CONTENTS

Produced by
Alfred Music Publishing Co., Inc.
P.O. Box 10003
Van Nuys, CA 91410-0003
alfred.com

Printed in USA.

ISBN-10: 0-7390-7213-7
ISBN-13: 978-0-7390-7213-4

Cover Christmas decorations: © istockphoto / filonmar

The Gift

Words and Music by Jim Brickman and Tom Douglas
Arr. Carol Tornquist

Jingle Bell Rock

Words and Music by Joe Beal and Jim Boothe
Arr. Carol Tornquist

Frosty the Snowman

Words and Music by Steve Nelson and Jack Rollins
Arr. Carol Tornquist

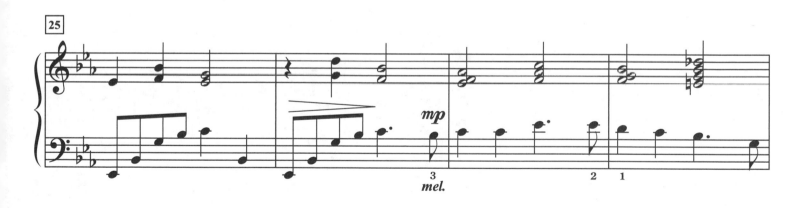

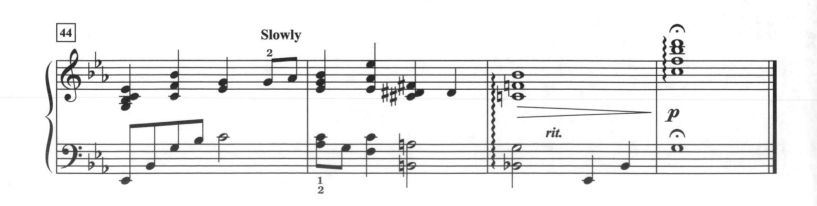

I'll Be Home for Christmas

Words by Kim Gannon
Music by Walter Kent
Arr. Carol Tornquist

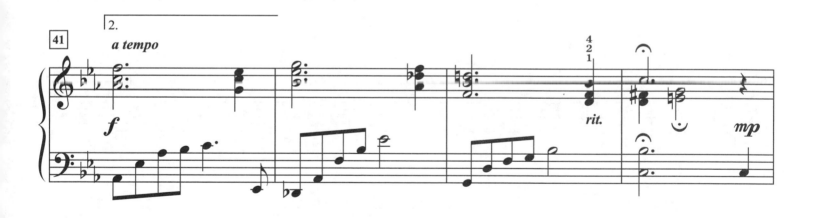

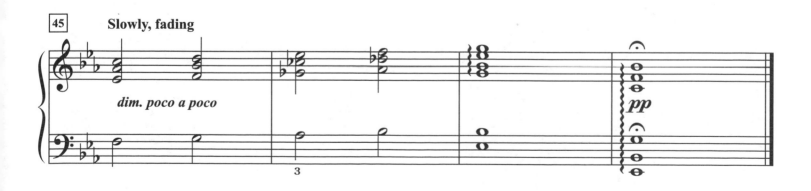

Santa Claus Is Comin' to Town

Words by Haven Gillespie
Music by J. Fred Coots
Arr. Carol Tornquist

The Christmas Waltz

Words by Sammy Cahn
Music by Jule Styne
Arr. Carol Tornquist

Moderately, with expression (♩ = 120)

Santa Baby

Words and Music by
Joan Javits, Philip Springer and Tony Springer
Arr. Carol Tornquist

GROWN-UP CHRISTMAS LIST

Words and Music by
David Foster and Linda Thompson Jenner
Arr. Carol Tornquist

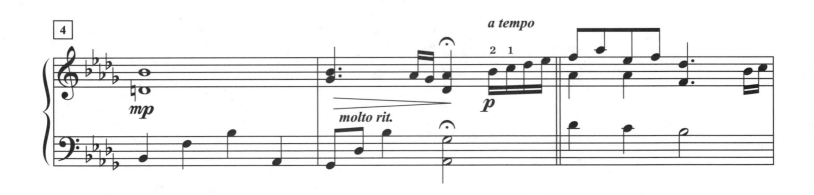

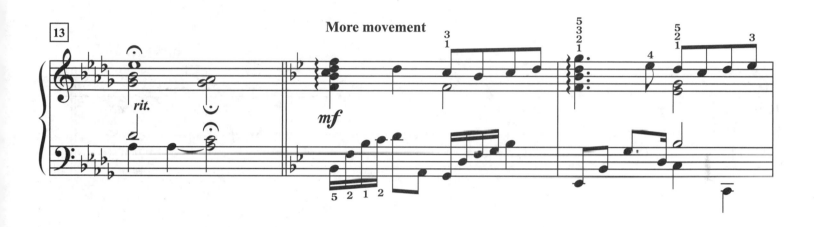

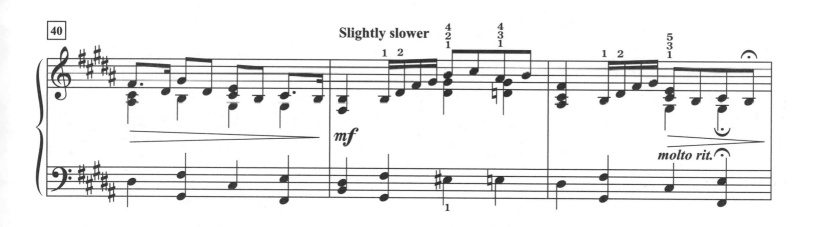

It's the Most Wonderful Time of the Year

Words and Music by Eddie Pola and George Wyle
Arr. Carol Tornquist

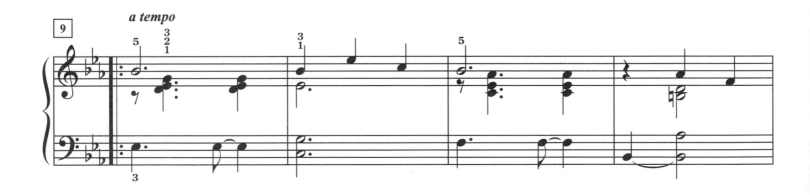

THE CHRISTMAS SHOES

Words and Music by Leonard Ahlstrom and Eddie Carswell
Arr. Carol Tornquist